THE 10 WAYS

THE 10 WAYS

A GUIDE TO THE 21ST CENTURY

RELATIONSHIP

Cynthia Chauvin

with *Miles Chauvin*

TWO DRAGONS

The 10 Ways
A Guide to the 21st Century Relationship
ISBN 13: 978-0-9816467-3-2

Cover Design by Jon Miles
Interior Design and Book Layout by DesignForBooks.com
Cover photography: Rubberball
Author photography: Joe Henson
Bebas font courtesy: Ryoichi Tsunekawa

Published by:
Two Dragons International Inc.
Washington D.C. | New Orleans
www.twodragons.com

For special pricing on bulk sales contact
booksales@twodragons.com

For more information and companion audio products please visit
Cynthia's website:
www.cynthiachauvin.com

To my Mr. Man

Acknowledgements

Thanks to the people who taught me I can't leave myself.

Thanks to my husband for helping me find myself.

Contents

Preface

Over the years in my practice as a psychic, I have read for thousands of women. I clock in at over 10,000 readings. In those thousands of readings, the most commonly asked questions were about relationships. No matter how the reading started, it always finished with questions about relationships.

If the woman was in a relationship, she asked: What do I need to do to make it better? Why doesn't he communicate? Can I trust him? Is he cheating? Why does he act so different now? Why did he change? Would I be better off ending it? Will he commit?

If the woman wasn't in a relationship, I heard: When will I meet him? What does he look like? What does he do? Will he be different from the last guy? Will it work out? Will it last?

Women who were newly broken up would ask: What went wrong? Why do I keep choosing losers? What was there to gain from this experience? Does he miss me? Is he sorry? Why didn't I listen to myself; I knew he was a schmuck! Why did he do blank? Does he feel bad about the way he treated me? Does he miss me? Is he seeing someone else? Did he move on?

Reading after reading, the message became clear. Women over-identified with their relationships as the source of their own value. How their partners behaved could make or destroy their day. When they had no partner, they obsessed about getting one.

Their resulting behavior ranged from controlling to cold and all the nuances in between. When they tried changing their behavior, they would do well until they placed themselves in a position that triggered their insecurity. This launched them straight back to their original destructive patterns.

No matter how much therapy or spiritual training they had, they were stuck in over-identification and the destructive behavior it causes. Even when they intellectually understood that they needed to be their own source of value, they could not make and maintain changes in their behavior.

Their behavior was not conducive to creating a relationship.

Because all permanent change starts in the subconscious, I began to offer hypnosis as well as psychic readings. I provided women not only with the When, Where, and Why answers they wanted, but the How. I taught them how to change the repetitive patterns in their relationships.

Those successful methods are represented in these few, very effective pages of knowledge gathered from thousands of women like you that sat in my chair asking, "Why?"

And then, invariably, "How?"

Introduction

If you are not yet satisfied with the relationships in your life (or there is a lack thereof), then you must look honestly at your thoughts, behavior, motivations and reactions, and discover what is driving them. Everyone has issues left over from childhood. But you are not a child any longer and you do not want your child-self running your relationships.

Deep inside you there is an adult-self capable of creating a solid, loving relationship with Mr. Man, and that's the self I am going to help you discover in this book. The path to your adult-self is being conscious, freeing your mind to an objective reality, and learning to understand your personal subjective one.

When you are clear about yourself, you will have the relationship you desire. Knowledge is power, and knowledge of self is the greatest power you can possess. Self-knowledge gives you the ability to choose rather than react. It gives you the ability to create based on the here and now, as opposed to the past.

Your life is the result of the tools you have used to create with thus far. If you are unhappy, then look at the tools you are using. What are they? Where did they come from? How might you change them?

This original tool set is the reason you keep creating the same experiences over and over in your relationships. Until you replace these tools, you will continue to create from the ones you developed somewhere between birth and early adolescence.

What follows are the instructions to build a new tool set for life—a life that includes a happy, healthy, intimate relationship with a loving and committed man. By the end of this book and the process it guides you through, this new tool set will have become part of you. In fact, it already is a part of you. You just need to solicit it.

The process is not about someone else (in other words, a man) or how he should change. It is about you and where your true power lies. It is not for those who wish to stay in a circular existence of re-creating old relationships, or for those who seek others to change in order to be happy.

This process is for women who want to grow. It is for women who want to become aware of their adult-selves, and who will take the steps necessary to accomplish a real relationship with themselves while seeking to connect with another. It is for women who want real and lasting change.

You can start at any time. If you are single, consider this a pre-flight checklist prior to takeoff. If you are married, consider this a way to make your flight first-class. If you are divorced, use the process to plan your next flight to a new and wonderful destination.

The principles in this book are universal. But for now, let's focus on you. Are you ready to embark on your journey? If so, here are your tools.

Right here, right now.

HOW TO USE THIS BOOK

Read each chapter twice, on two consecutive days (for instance, a Monday and a Tuesday). Then use the Practice Time exercise you find at the end of the chapter for the following five days (in this case, Wednesday through Sunday). That means you'll be spending a total of seven days working on the material in each chapter.

As tempting as it may be to do so, don't jump ahead. Be sure to take an entire week for each chapter's learning to solidify. The later chapters build on the earlier chapters. When you build a house, you want to be sure the foundation is solid before building the next floor. The same is true here.

One layer of this book is designed to speak directly to your conscious mind. Another layer speaks directly to your subconscious mind. To make change, you have to work with both layers. To understand the relationship of the conscious and subconscious mind, think of an iceberg. Only 10 percent of an iceberg is visible above water. Ninety percent is under the surface. This book speaks to both the conscious mind on top and the subconscious mind underneath.

As you go through the chapters, you will have realizations about your life and behavior. At the same time, you will notice your emotions naturally realigning without any effort. This means the process is working.

WORKING ALONE OR IN A GROUP

You can do the work in this book on your own. Or you can work with an open and honest girlfriend or a group of girlfriends who you trust and admire. If you choose to work with others, try to pick positive people.

Do this process as many times as you want. You will find new layers as you change and grow in your life.

1

Own Your Behavior

I f you have been through relationship after relation-ship where you find yourself repeating the same arguments, experiences and drama, understand that the common denominator is you. And for you to have a different kind of relationship, what you need to change is you—more specifically, the part of you that is in charge of your current world and personal views.

Many different parts of you influence your behavior on an array of subjects. You created most of these parts in order to survive childhood experiences, and all of them have a positive intent, such as keeping you safe.

Let's call these parts "The Little Girl." She comes in a variety of behavior patterns: pleasing, obedient, rebellious, contrary, cooperative. This list goes on and on. The problem is that these parts use antiquated behavior.

Such is the case with The Little Girl part that tries to control her future outcome by controlling your behavior (and the behavior of others) using the language of shame and blame. Her pattern is one that I like to call The Shame-Blame Game.

The Shame-Blame Game is learned during childhood when our moms, dads, teachers, and other adults used it to obtain a particular behavior from us. They learned it from the adults in their childhood. The irony is this is not adult behavior. It never was and it never will be. It is a child's behavior passed from generation to generation.

The Shame-Blame Game is not introspective thinking. It is not going over the events to create change. It does not include positive dialogue with yourself or with Mr. Man.

There are two basic types of shame-blame: internal and external.

In the internal Shame-Blame Game, you shame and blame yourself, resulting in a never-ending cycle of self-criticism.

Here's an example of an internal shame dialogue: You are in a relationship with Mr. Man and something just doesn't feel right. You say to yourself, "It must be my imagination. I am reading too much into it." When he turns out to be a less than wonderful Mr. Wonderful, you're embarrassed and think to yourself, "Why didn't I see this coming? Why didn't I listen to myself?"

In an attempt to control a reoccurrence of this event, you shame yourself so you do not ignore or overlook warning signs again. You promise yourself that next time the outcome will be different.

Here's an example of an internal blame dialogue: Your partner leaves you because he says you are too cold and withdrawn. You think, "He was so perfect. He could have been the one." Angry with yourself, you think, "Why didn't I show him more warmth, more of my true self?"

In an attempt to control a reoccurrence of this event, you blame yourself for acting withdrawn and losing a potentially good relationship. You promise yourself that next time the outcome will be different.

In the external or projected Shame-Blame Game, you shame and blame your partner, resulting in a never-ending cycle of criticism.

Here's an example of an external shame dialogue: You are dating Mr. Man and he forgets to attend your company function. Feeling humiliated and embarrassed, you think to yourself, "He is so inconsiderate. I am not important to him."

That evening he apologizes, but nothing he says is good enough to make up for his transgression. Doing your best to make him feel bad, you say, "I can't believe you would do this to me. I don't understand how you could be so insensitive."

In an attempt to control a reoccurrence of this event, you shame him so he will never forget you again. You want him to promise that next time the outcome will be different.

Here's an example of an external blame dialogue: You think you have caught your Mr. Man in a lie. He tells you he is going one place, only you find him at another—and he is not alone. Assuming the worst, you feel betrayed and think, "I knew it, he's cheating. He's been lying to me all along." You confront him in anger.

Although his explanation is perfectly reasonable, you blame him for your emotional outburst, saying, "This is all your fault, I never act this way. You should have told me your plans changed. What did you expect me to do finding you with someone else?"

In an attempt to control a reoccurrence of this event, you blame him for your outburst of anger. You want him to promise that next time the outcome will be different.

In reality, women mix the different ingredients of The Shame-Blame Game until they have a shame-blame jambalaya.

Are you playing the Shame-Blame Game now in some part of your life?

Do you feel shame about ignoring the actions of a partner? Do you blame yourself when things don't work out and immediately think, if I had only done "X" things would be different?

Have you tried to shame a man to get what you want? Did you react to a man's behavior and then blame him for your behavior and choices?

The next time you find yourself in a situation that stimulates any form of a shame-blame dialogue, close your eyes and ask yourself, "Who is doing the talking?" Is it your adult-self, or The Little Girl? Most likely, you will find your disappointed little girl is in charge.

Do you really want to give The Little Girl dominion over your life? Would you let her buy a house, take a new job, start a business, or have access to your bank account? Of course not, but you probably already do. You probably give The Little Girl autonomy in many more places than you like to admit.

The Shame-Blame Game can permeate many aspects of your life. While it may seem like an effective strategy, it is not. It is the strategy of an insecure child trying to control outcomes. It is not the best strategy for a good relationship.

The Shame-Blame Game throws you and Mr. Man straight back to childhood, creating a relationship based on all the unresolved childhood issues associated with shame and blame. Ultimately it leads one or both parties to rebellion, or worse yet, compliance.

There is hope. You *can* change the repetitive Shame-Blame Game.

How? By owning your behavior.

The next time you feel an attack of The Shame-Blame Game coming your way, prior to spewing words like Niagara Falls, take a moment. In this moment you can change your world permanently. This moment holds your creative potential. It is your doorway to change in your relationships.

The most liberating thing you can choose in this moment is curiosity. Curiosity does not hold judgment. It is the key to a good relationship. When you are curious, your mind can solicit answers about your feelings and behavior.

Between stimulus and response there is a space. In that space is our power to choose our response. In our response lies our growth and our freedom.

—Viktor E. Frankl

The best place to solicit answers is to engage in a conversation with your "Objective Viewer." Your Objective Viewer is your inner wise woman, your *adult-self*. She is the pathway to your personal wisdom. She is your greatest ally in life.

The Shame-Blame Game depletes your ability to see your own life clearly. This keeps your Objective Viewer a small voice in the distance, only able to guide you in the manner your consciousness will allow. She waits for you to become curious and change your focus from others to self. Without your Objective Viewer, you see the world passively through your life experiences projected like a movie onto the life of another.

Your Objective Viewer sees the entirety of your life without judgment. She supplies you with answers to your questions, such as: What is really concerning me about this situation? What am I feeling and have I felt this way before? Am I sabotaging this relationship?

Your Objective Viewer is there to answer your questions and show you that you are not your experiences and behavior. Solicit her and follow her down the path of self-awareness. You will live a life of discovery, possibility, and potential.

Your Objective Viewer, your Inner Wise Woman, is uniquely yours. Imagine what she looks like. She may resemble one of your teachers or be a mix of you and a favorite relative. She can be younger, older, happy, or elegant. She can be dressed in royal robes, have the presence of a warm fire, or sound like an angel's choir. How you imagine her is up to you.

Once you have open communication with your Objective Viewer, she will help you own your life as your creation and thereby you will Own Your Behavior.

Ownership is a powerful position to adopt, because you cannot change what you did not create. So, when you have consciously accepted responsibility for your life, you can expand old thoughts and create new out-comes.

Your thoughts are your energy, here to service you. When you combine your thoughts with emotions, intense focus, and repetition, you manifest. For better or worse, your thoughts are a magnet for creation. The thoughts you are having right now are your life in the making.

Ask yourself, "Am I using my thoughts, my energy, to create for my highest good, my highest expression of love?" "Are my motives pure?" If not, start again. You already tried controlling yourself and others with the Shame-Blame Game, which is how you lost your power to begin with.

Making a choice to be curious today brings back a piece of your energy that was put to sleep by The Shame-Blame Game. When you are curious and see your life objectively, your behavior will change. You will claim your power to direct your life.

Owning your behavior is how to get and keep your man.

EVERY DAY, IMAGINE A NEW YOU

Practice the following exercise every day for the next five days.

Practice giving yourself automatic new resources when you need them, resources to help you make the changes you want in your life.

Take one of your oldest Shame-Blame Games—one you want to change. Then, close your eyes and imagine a movie screen in front of you. On this screen, see yourself in the most recent scene where you used this behavior.

Describe it aloud. Include everything: what it looks like, feels like, smells like. What are you wearing? What do your surroundings look like? Feel the emotions you had in that scene.

In a corner of the movie screen, see a small white square. Let the white square take over your scene inch by inch, until the screen is completely white and blank. Repeat three times, each time faster than the last.

Next, work with your Objective Viewer to make an image of how you would like to behave in the future. See yourself at your best: self-confident, competent, and resourceful. This image is your new self. Make your new self as vivid as possible.

Place this image of your confident, competent, and resourceful new self in the background of your scene. (This means the past scene is in front and the new self is in the back). Move your new self forward, becoming brighter as the past scene moves to the background, becoming dimmer. Let your new self fill the scene. Repeat three times, each time faster than the last.

Finally, take the new self and place it in the left-hand corner of a blank white movie screen. Let the new self take over the screen. See the new self become brighter, more vivid, and more alive. Repeat three times, each time faster than the last one.

For the next five mornings, before
you get out of bed, list one thing in
a journal for which you are grateful.

MORNING *I am grateful for...*

DAY 1

1.
_____

DAY 2

1.
_____

DAY 3

1.
_____

DAY 4

1.
_____

DAY 5

1.
_____

For the next five evenings, before bed, list one thing you like about yourself.

EVENING *I am...*

DAY 1

1.

DAY 2

1.

DAY 3

1.

DAY 4

1.

DAY 5

1.

2

Create a New Value System

Through your family of origin you are born into the world of experience. Your experiences with your family and with society form your internalized family value system. This system becomes the foundation from which you create. Each experience in your life is judged good or bad against this framework.

Here is a hypothetical example of a family value system at work. Your mom says, "In a perfect marriage, the woman is beautiful and the man is rich." So you go through life with these unrealistic expectations.

You obsess over every perceived personal flaw while constantly looking for the "perfect" wealthy man.

You also have the larger family of society speaking into your ear. For example, the community around you might say, "The only road to happiness is to get married, have children, a successful career, and a dog or cat." Because of this, if you don't have these things, you think something is missing.

In essence, any relationship you have is based on and judged against the original relationship you had with your family and society. Your relationships become independent of your family of origin and societal experience when your value system becomes independent.

It does not matter how many things you change about yourself (for example, your appearance, career, education, or mantras). It does not matter how much work you do on yourself psychologically, intellectually, spiritually, or physically. Until you change your value system, your relationships will turn out basically the same.

This is what your family value system looks like. You think, you want a man like blank and the order is filled by the universal system of cause and effect. However, your family value system—your foundation—determines the kind of man you get, not your external statements.

The world of cause and effect produces the actions necessary to create what has already been chosen from your family value system. For example, if a highly critical person influenced you as a child, your inherent family value system will recreate a relationship with a man who is critical in your adulthood.

The new man you thought you asked for does not show up. Instead, the old type appears over and over again. You continue building new relationships from old thoughts about yourself while expecting a different outcome, creating a status quo. Doing the same thing and expecting a different outcome is nutso.

The status quo of your family value system is primarily held in place by repetitively questioning your past. Asking yourself questions such as "Why is my mom so cold to me?" "Why did my dad leave me?" and "Why me, why me, why did this happen to me?" just reinforce the original value system that you create your life and relationships from.

These are not the type of Why questions that would expand and develop you, or create change in you. This

Why does not come from a place of innocence and curiosity. This Why seeks to blame. It actually perpetuates the drama you seek to avoid. It keeps your family value system alive and well.

But you may think, "If only I knew why he left me, then I would feel better." This is what I like to call "Why Insurance." It is looking for an answer to avoid experiencing the situation again. But behind every Why there is another Why, and then another, and another.

This status quo Why needs to be eliminated from your life.

Using this toxic Why in conversation with another person is just as harmful as using it with yourself. Asking "Why did you do that?" maneuvers a person into giving an answer that you may then criticize, keeping you in the same cycle.

Even when given an answer, you will not feel better because you are looking for an answer that makes you feel safe. Another person's answer to Why is never as good as yours. There is no Why that can satisfy.

You must transcend the question Why.

Your family value system is based on your childhood memory of experiences, coated with new and ongoing emotions, bringing about a tainted vision of your worth—whether good or bad. This is not your value.

Your Spirit is your true value system.

Your Spirit knows that no experience should come before it. When you make your experiences your value, you have made the experiences more important than your Spirit. When you let your experiences define your behavior, you make the experiences your god. You place a false god before you.

Your Spirit is not mesmerized by your experiences, hypnotized by your emotions, and attached to your joy or pain for its identity. Your Spirit values no experience as your worth. Your Spirit is limitless possibilities and potential. Your Spirit does not need to know Why.

You can create a new value system by reclaiming your Spirit, your endless possibilities, and your endless potential the minute you are willing to stand in a Why-free zone.

From this zone you are free to create your love, your relationships, and your life.

PEOPLE AND HABIT DIET/NEW VALUE SYSTEM

Practice the following exercise every day for the next five days. This exercise has two parts.

PART 1 *Disconnect from Your Old Family Value System*

Go on a people and habit diet. Don't socialize with your regular entourage, including people at work (if it is possible to avoid them). Don't engage in your normal conversations with anyone. Don't watch your regular television program. Don't read your normal choice in literature. Do nothing the same and do nothing with the same people, including family. Disconnect in as many places as you can.

This is powerful. It will lead you to change. Be on guard, your entourage will attempt to bring you back into the fold.

PART 2 *Connect to Your New Spiritual Value System*

With your newly available time observe the magnificent world you live in. Meditate or pray in whatever way works for you. Seek out nature in your area. Be observant of the sky, the trees, and the wildlife. For example, if you live in the desert, be observant of the cactus. Don't just look. Take time to think, feel, and smell. Close your eyes and absorb the magnificence.

The magnificence of the Earth is unparalleled. The ocean, mountains, desert, and rivers stand in brilliant harmony with each other. Recognize that you are made of the same elements as this great and beautiful planet. You are created in perfection. Recognize that perfection.

Does the Earth have a problem being its most magnificent self? No. Does the sky have a problem lighting the night with an abundance of brilliant shining stars? No. Does the Grand Canyon have a problem being grand? No. Does the ocean have a problem being untamable, wild and powerful? No. Does a bird have a problem spreading its wings and flying? Absolutely no.

The Earth and the skies don't need approval to shine. Neither do you.

This week, if you find yourself doubting your value, pause and remind yourself that you are allowing old experiences to devalue your Spirit. Focus on nature and connect to it, and say this mantra aloud several times as a quick way to rebalance your self:

"My spirit is my true value."

For the next five mornings, before you get out of bed, list two things for which you are grateful.

MORNING   *I am grateful for...*

DAY 1

1.

2.

DAY 2

1.

2.

DAY 3

1.

2.

DAY 4

1. _____

_____

2. _____

_____

DAY 5

1. _____

_____

2. _____

_____

For the next five evenings, before bed, list two things you like about yourself.

EVENING *I am...*

DAY 1

1.

2.

DAY 2

1.

2.

DAY 3

1.

2.

DAY 4

1. _____

_____

2. _____

_____

DAY 5

1. _____

_____

2. _____

_____

3

Start with Self-Communication

Good communication starts with good self-communication. Communication with the self is a life-long love affair.

Most people avoid communicating with themselves and go straight to someone else to validate their position. They look to others for answers to their questions, relying on someone else's view of the world. They look for someone to reinforce what they think.

This form of validation never works.

Instead of trying to find your clone, start communication with the person who knows you better than anyone. No one knows you better than you. You are the expert of your life.

Self-communication begins when you depend on yourself for your answers and only see external stimulus as an expression of your internal process.

Self-communication is not self-talk.

Self-talk is an unhelpful inner dialogue that is ready to deliver the same results you have already experienced. It is created from your family and society value system, and labels your experiences as good or bad. Self-talk is easy to recognize because its voice is usually judgmental.

Self-talk can be negative or unrealistically positive in its voice. It can sound like, "What is wrong with me? I am so stupid" or "I am just too good for him." Self-talk originates in your past, comes through your subconscious, and plays its message in your head without your permission.

The good news is the subconscious can be reprogrammed. That is the voice you began relinquishing in last week's exercises.

Members of the groups you associate with usually hold similar opinions on reality, thereby supporting your family value system and enhancing your self-talk. You hold yourself in line by inserting into your inner dialogue the commentary of religious groups, cultural groups, political groups, charitable groups, and groups of friends.

Some groups you join at birth, others you join later. It doesn't matter whether you are in rebellion or in acceptance of the experience. You can love your family or hate your family—both perpetuate the illusion that your experience creates your self-worth, which in turn creates your self-talk.

For example, if a family believes that a woman who is unmarried at 35 will never marry, her self-talk could sound like this: "I am never going to be married." "I will always be alone." "No one is going to want someone my age."

Self-talk influenced by society could sound like this: "My breasts are too small." "My thighs are too big." "Pretty women are never taken seriously." "I don't have a man because men are intimidated by me." "No one wants me because I am not perfect." "I am too perfect for them."

It's time to tune out self-talk.

The antidote to self-talk is your Objective Viewer, so put her to use. She has complete access to your intelligence and personal history. She has all your answers.

Let your Objective Viewer satisfy your need to be heard. She will put everything in context. For example, if you are projecting your fear of getting hurt into a new relationship (causing you to be aloof and skeptical), then your Objective Viewer can listen to your fears. She can remind you that this is a different man and you can trust yourself to know when it is safe to open your heart.

And if you are making assumptions about his behavior and reading your own meaning into his actions (such as when he is not calling as much, assuming he must be pulling away), then your Objective Viewer can listen to your concerns and remind you to clarify his intent with curiosity.

Once you have solid self-communication and you have tuned out self-talk, you can communicate effectively even with the poorest of communicators. You can have beautiful relationships with anyone if you know how to communicate properly with yourself. And in the presence of a good communicator, even the poorest communicators find themselves being articulate in ways they have never been before. They feel safe to be themselves.

We've all been around that person who is easy to talk to and who makes us feel comfortable. It's your turn to be that person. Here's how.

A good communicator owns her fears and hurts. She does not project her emotions onto another person. For example, she does not take her anger about herself or someone else out on the person in front of her. She can express her emotions honestly and listen to other people talk about their emotions without rejecting them.

A good communicator speaks with clarity. She listens without judgment. She does not abandon her opinions for other people's acceptance. She holds to her own views while being open to other perspectives. This is power. This allows her to hear the other person, even the one who says little.

A good communicator never assumes the other person understands the meaning of what she is saying, nor does she assume she understands their meaning. She knows that the word "apple" might mean a Red Delicious apple to one person and a Granny Smith tart green apple to another. A good communicator gently clarifies what she is saying.

It sounds like this: "Please let me clarify what I am saying. It is like blank" (giving an example the other person can relate to). When you use a common metaphor to clarify what you are saying, people relate very quickly.

A good communicator also gently clarifies what she is hearing. It sounds like this: "Am I understanding you correctly? Do you mean blank?" Parrot back what you thought you heard as close to the other person's words as possible.

If you are on the same page, stop there. If you don't understand, seek clarity with curiosity. It sounds like this: "Would you expand on your thought? I am curious, what do you mean when you say blank?"

A good communicator holds the person in front of her in unconditional positive regard. Unconditional positive regard is a powerful tool. It is a sign of being in the present. When you are emanating unconditional positive regard, clarity, and lack of personal agenda, you have the basis for true communication with your Mr. Man.

INFINITE POSSIBILITIES

Practice the following exercise every day for the next five days.

Infinite Possibilities is an exercise that helps you put your past where it belongs: in the past. You can use it anytime you desire insight about your feelings, emotions, or behavior. It will help you find and implement alternative responses in any situation.

Example: You are upset because his apple is green and yours is red. Maybe you picked another loser. He looked like he had so much potential.

Stop! Do the following.

Close your eyes and imagine your present-self drifting out of your body. Joining you is your Objective Viewer, who sees everything clearly.

Imagine you are hovering above yourself. Below you can see your life in a straight horizontal line. Along the line in one direction is the past: the good times, the other times, holidays, birthdays, work, and fun, all the way back to your birth. In the other direction is the future: your dreams, your potential, and where you'd like to go in life.

Ask your Objective Viewer to take you to a time in the past that is connected to the emotions at hand. Watch both of you float down your timeline until you come to a place where she stops. Take some time to view the situation below. Don't force any particular image; simply work with what is presented.

Float down to the scene and introduce yourself and your Objective Viewer to your past you. Make friends with her. Tell her you are from her future and you are here to help. Ask her the positive intent of her feelings, emotions, and behavior. For what purpose does she use them? Tell her she has done a wonderful job, and you would like to give her new possibilities to use when she feels called upon to react to this type of situation.

If your past self doesn't understand, continue assuring her that she has done a good job. Offer to show her different ways to handle the situation.

Once you get a yes—and you will get a yes—use your imagination to think of new ways to view and respond to the situation. Suggest them to the past you, as an alternative to the behavior she uses when she feels threatened. Agree on three or four new ways and look for a sign of agreement, such as a feeling, a nod, or a wink.

Then tell her that, along with these new possibilities, you have a great gift for her, a bag of infinite possibilities that she can use any time she needs more options. Hand her a bag filled with glowing, glittering possibilities. This bag will automatically generate new possibilities whenever she needs them.

Also let the past you know that along with all these new ways to see the situation, she has full access to you and your Objective Viewer anytime she needs help. She can call upon both of you for help in any situation.

Have a big hug. Then float out of the scene, travel back to the present and get back inside your body. You have just communicated with yourself, your behavior, your feelings, and your emotions—and with the only person who knows what you mean when you say "apple."

For the next five mornings, before
you get out of bed, list three
things for which you are grateful.

MORNING *I am grateful for...*

DAY 1

1.

2.

3.

DAY 2

1.

2.

3.

DAY 3

1. _____
   _____

2. _____
   _____

3. _____
   _____

DAY 4

1. _____
   _____

2. _____
   _____

3. _____
   _____

DAY 5

1. _____
   _____

2. _____
   _____

3. _____
   _____

*For the next five evenings, before
bed, list three things you like
about yourself.*

EVENING   *I am...*

DAY 1

1.

2.

3.

DAY 2

1.

2.

3.

DAY 3

1.

2.

3.

DAY 4

1.

2.

3.

DAY 5

1.

2.

3.

4

Commit to Living Your Life

I just can't find a man ready to commit." You have heard it and you have said it.

If you can't find a Mr. Man who wants to commit, or you continually find reasons why you can't commit to a relationship, the issue is you. You have a problem committing and your experiences with men reflect this.

Question: Do you continually up the ante in arguments, finding fault at every turn? Is the grass always greener on the other side of the fence? Do you leave for a better lawn, which turns out to have just as much dog poop on it as the last one? Do you pick a new Mr. Man expecting a different outcome, only to find yourself in the same place you were with the last Mr. Man?

You are the non-committer.

You might reply, "Yes, but if he asked me to marry him I'd say yes—it's his problem." No, it's your problem for being in a relationship with a man who won't ask you. If you commit to a man or to a series of men who won't commit to you, you are committed to non-commitment.

It's your problem. Get over the shock waves.

No longer can you say, "I just can't find someone willing to commit" or "I can't find the right one to commit to." You must say, "I have a problem with commitment."

Fear is the reason many women are not able to commit. The fear can be manifested from an experience of loss, betrayal, or being left. Women also fear they will pick the wrong guy and be stuck with Mr. Wrong when Mr. Right shows up. They are trying to avoid a bad decision, which leads to no decision. Which is an active decision to avoid commitment.

There are also passive ways to avoid commitment. A classic passive technique is patiently waiting for Mr. Man to make a decision to commit.

Sound familiar?

When a woman patiently waits for Mr. Man to make a decision to commit, her pseudo-patience turns into resentment, even when the outcome is his commitment.

Don't be "patient."

"Patience" holds energy in place against its natural tendency. Life is moving. Resentment can't grow in the moving energy of life.

You must move forward and live your life. You don't have to be aware of all your commitment issues or conquer your fears to do this.

Conquering fear is like counting sand on a beach, with each grain of sand representing a reason. It's an impossible task, because the reasons, like grains of sand, are constantly shifting. If you like to dig on the beach because you believe you can't change your problem without knowing its origin, then dig away.

Just don't believe you will dig until you come to some cathartic moment that will remove all your blocks about being in a relationship. You may have that cathartic moment, but experience holds that once you have the moment, there is another one and another one. Before long you have dug from Destin Beach,

Florida, to Santa Monica, California. Get off the beach.

Life is not static and it's not an intellectual exercise. Living life is how you commit to life and Mr. Man.

CLIENT STORY

I vividly remember having a conversation with a client who called about her Mr. Man. She expressed how much she loved and cherished him, but he wasn't able to make a commitment to her. He was open and honest about his inability to commit and his desire to have multiple relationships.

"Take him at is word," I said. "He is not ready to commit. He will work his issues out. In a couple of years he will be ready for a bona fide faithful commitment for life, without other people in the background." However, I knew the problem was hers.

I explained to her that she was a passive non-committer. She had pulled in someone that gave her the ability not to commit. I suggested she stop focusing on his commitment problem and work on her own.

Going further I warned, "Do not have so-called patience, do not wait to live your life. Stay open to other relationships. If you find someone of interest, pursue it. Do not shut down to life, live it. Live your life." And I added, "Do not sleep with him unless you are all right with him sleeping with other women."

My recommendation was that she see him if she wanted to, but without judgment of his process. I told her she had the choice to see him or not, but not the choice to change him.

My counsel was not to wait for him with the false belief that she was waiting for what she wanted, because she wouldn't want it when she got it. If she "sacrificed" her time waiting for him, she would resent him. I told her she should not hold him accountable for her decision to wait. This was her way not to commit.

Over the years I had many calls with her where I reiterated the same message: "Live your life. Don't wait. You are using him to avoid your issue of non-commitment."

Without fail, her Mr. Man came to the end of his road and said to her, "I love you. I have always loved you. I was afraid of getting hurt, and I realize not committing is not keeping me safe."

Then he proposed.

Her response? "I just can't marry you after what you have done to me over the past few years."

He had gotten over his non-commitment by living his life. She had stayed in non-commitment by not living hers, all the while using pseudo-patience to build resentment in order not to commit—yet again.

To recognize you have the problem of non-commitment is the biggest part of the solution. Ownership is your salvation. Ownership of your seen and unseen behavior will set you free. Once it is yours, you can change the wiring that causes your repetitive behavior of non-commitment.

Non-commitment is a survival program created by a part of you that you have long since forgotten. Rewiring and changing your programming makes new thoughts bigger, fuller and more alive than your old thoughts. So let's change your root thoughts about commitment right now and set you free to commit to living your life.

TOOTH BRUSH MANTRA

Practice the following exercise every day for the next five days.

Your present-day thoughts are past thoughts out of which you created a belief system for your survival. This survival system has repeated itself over and over in your life. This repetition has hypnotized you into an automatic behavior.

To repeat, this behavior is automatic.

Since it was your belief system that hypnotized you into repetitive thoughts, and since these thoughts created your behavior in regards to commitment, let's use self-hypnosis to create new thoughts about commitment.

While you are brushing your teeth in the morning and evening, stare deeply into the mirror and repeat (in your mind): "I am one with Love. Love and I are one."

It is important that you do this while looking in the mirror. Remember to look into your eyes.

After you have finished brushing your teeth, return to looking at yourself in the mirror and repeat the same mantra out loud three more times.

Why use such a simple mantra?

If it is easy, you will use it. When rewiring your mind, a few powerful words are better than lengthy postulations and affirmations.

Why repeat, "I am one with Love. Love and I are one" and not "I am not afraid to commit?" Because "I am not afraid to commit" carries "I *am afraid* to commit" within its statement. On the other hand, "I am one with Love. Love and I are one" has no negative word in it (no *not*).

It is important that you expand your thoughts from the positive. Love must be your programming; all things grow from love.

This mantra has nothing to do with getting love, giving love, or sharing love.

This is about being Love.

For the next five mornings, before you get out of bed, list four things for which you are grateful.

MORNING *I am grateful for...*

DAY 1

1.

2.

3.

4.

DAY 2

1.

2.

3. _____
   _____
   _____

4. _____
   _____
   _____

DAY 3

1. _____
   _____
   _____

2. _____
   _____
   _____

3. _____
   _____
   _____

4. _____
   _____
   _____

DAY 4

1. _____
   _____
   _____

2. _____
   _____
   _____

3. _____
   _____
   _____

4.

DAY 5

1.

2.

3.

4.

For the next five evenings, before bed, list four things you like about yourself.

EVENING   *I am...*

DAY 1

1.

2.

3.

4.

DAY 2

1.

2.

3.

_____

_____

4.

_____

_____

DAY 3

1.

_____

_____

2.

_____

_____

3.

_____

_____

4.

_____

_____

DAY 4

1.

_____

_____

2.

_____

_____

3.

_____

_____

4.

_____

_____

DAY 5

1.

_____

_____

2.

_____

_____

3.

_____

_____

4.

_____

_____

5

Pick Your Time

D o you fall short on taking time before you respond? Do you use counting to ten as added time to line up a blast of criticism or self-defense? Have you ever said or thought, "I have to tell him what I think right *now!* "

A PERSONAL STORY

One day my friend Norma told me about her boyfriend making a hurtful remark at dinner the night before. When she confided in me, I responded, "Did you tell him how you feel?" I was 23 and absolutely undone by his callous treatment of my good friend.

"No." she said.

I immediately retorted, "You need to call him and tell him what an ass he has been." It's likely my vocabulary was much more colorful.

She said, "I didn't address this with him last night, nor am I going to address this with him today. He is not in a place to hear me and I am not in a place to say what I really want to say." She paused, and then continued, "I will pick my time."

"Pick your time?" I said. "How can you pick your time? What about the need to say something, anything, right now so you can get it off your chest?"

Norma just looked at me and said, "It would not be an effective use of my energy." Continuing, Norma dropped the big bomb, "We had a wonderful evening together."

At the time, I thought Norma was nuts. Now, I think the chick had her shit together big time.

Norma was able to compartmentalize her moment of hurt and allow the rest of the evening to go untouched.

She did not have to make the entire evening bad. She knew that when you turn a whole evening over to getting your point across, no point is made.

She could do this because she was in charge of her emotions. The part of her that was upset knew she would take care of business at the right time, so her emotions didn't have to boil over then and there. Her emotions were under her admirable control. Not the other way around.

Norma also made the astute observation that her boyfriend was generally a pleasant guy and must have been in a bad place to say such a hurtful comment.

Norma's method of "pick your time" made several things possible that would not have been possible with an immediate emotional response.

First, she had the time to process and come to terms with what the situation meant to her. Second, she had the time to reflect on what his comment may have meant to him. Third, she aligned herself with curiosity to inquire from him what he meant. Then she used her observational resources to choose what she wanted to express.

Norma handled herself like a true master painter. She created a beautiful picture of curiosity and observation, which allowed her to direct her thoughts and energy into true communication.

Wahoo! That is true art.

It took me years to see the advantage of taking time to respond. Now I am here to tell you that picking your time is a powerhouse resource you should use everywhere.

Of course, like any resource, picking your time can be used for good or not so good. Never use the "pick your time" method to align yourself with more resources to humiliate, build a case against, shame, blame, guilt, or any other method you may be accustomed to using to prove your point.

The cost is too great.

The person you are trying to communicate with loses trust and begins to build up radar to cut you off before you begin to speak. This compromises all healthy communication. You are never heard and nothing ever changes, all for the glory of a few random jabs by The Little Girl.

Knowledge is power. Use it wisely. Use it to better yourself. You will be happier with the results, and the results will be much more effective. So if you are currently picking your time to castrate your loved one, remember you are doing so at the cost of being heard, making change, and living a life in harmony.

Whatever you do to Mr. Man, you do to yourself and the relationship. This is an ultimate truth. Play with this at your peril. No matter how you couch the words, "I just want to be heard," if it entails belittling him, it will cost you just that—being heard.

Use the Force like Yoda, not like Darth Vader.

When Mr. Man puts his foot in his mouth, don't jump to a conclusion. Take your time. Enjoy the rest of the evening. Later, look over your thoughts and feelings with your Objective Viewer. She will help you. She can move you out of your emotions and your intellect and into the higher perspective of the intuitive self. Once you have this perspective, approach your man with curiosity to elicit his thoughts and articulate your feelings without shame or blame.

You may be thinking, "Yeah right. I could never do that."

How or why Norma innately knew how to do this is anyone's guess. Maybe it grew from her experiences. Maybe she was just so endowed. Maybe it came from another life.

I am here to tell you that this is possible. You can develop this attribute of choosing your response because what one woman can do, another can do.

YOU-NIVERSAL REMOTE

Practice the following exercise every day for the next five days.

Let's "Normafy" your impulse to respond by using a new tool: the "You-niversal Remote."

Most people don't realize their behavior is rehearsed through repetition, so when they try to implement a new un-rehearsed behavior, it fails.

The more you rehearse a new behavior, the more the behavior becomes part of your subconscious. And the more you use it, the faster, easier, and more natural it will become. This is how your reactions became as fast as they are. They were rehearsed so many times that they became automatic, even when they were not good for you.

This process is not about "changing" who you are; it's about growing and expanding who you are beyond your present subconscious self-talk.

To end longstanding bad behavior, you need a tool. A television remote is an exceedingly helpful visual tool. We've all held a remote. Everyone has pressed the pause button while watching a movie. You can pause, rewind, or fast-forward anything in your life the same way you can with a remote control.

Practice makes perfect, so let's practice. Imagine your You-Niversal Remote in your hand. You can use an actual remote if that helps with the visualization.

Envision a past situation with a lover, one where your assumption about his behavior was wrong and as a result of your assumption a joyful evening was replaced by a nightmare on Elm Street.

Imagine this scene in a vivid manner. Use your senses. Put yourself there. What were you wearing? What perfume did you have on? What color were your shoes? What did he exactly say? Or, in my case, what color hair did I have? See yourself just about to head down the road of no return.

Before your emotions fully bloom, hit pause and freeze the scene. Make the scene black and white, turn off the volume and fast-forward through your emotions, knowing you can, and will, take time to look at this moment when you have better resources to view it with. See the rest of the scene as if you had fast-forwarded through your emotions and had a beautiful evening.

Do this several times using the same scene or different ones all using your imagination vividly. With each time, fast-forward even more quickly. By the last time you do this exercise, you have fast-forwarded past your negative emotions so quickly that they are just a blip.

Let's move to the future.

Imagine a future situation where you are having a good time with a new Mr. Man. Everything is flowing. See the scene vividly. Again, use your senses. Feel the clothes on your skin. Hear the room noise.

Imagine he says something that strikes at your ego. Just as your head is about to spin, hit pause, freezing the scene before the emotion zings at your body, while you still have your wits about you.

Make the scene black and white, turn off the volume and fast-forward through your emotions. Know you can and will take time to look at this moment when you have better resources to view it with. At the end of the scene, see the two of you carrying on a beautiful, romantic, passionate evening.

Practice the use of your You-niversal Remote in situations with your friends, family, employees, or boss. The more you use it in your life, the better able you will be to use it when you are in front of Mr. Man. Whenever you have an uncomfortable feeling, hit that pause button on your You-niversal Remote and fast-forward past your emotions and assumptions. Blip!

Don't forget that the paused moment must be attended to. Be sure to follow through with personal reflection using the Objective Viewer. Choose how you wish to express this insight, if at all. Always align yourself with curiosity before you make an inquiry of Mr. Man.

From this point on, every time you see a remote control, you will be pleasantly reminded of your ability to manage your emotions. Every time you see a remote, this tool set will be pushed deeper and deeper into your subconscious mind. Your behavior will be automatically "Normafied."

From this moment on, you are blessed with this power.

For the next five mornings, before
you get out of bed, list five things
for which you are grateful.

MORNING *I am grateful for...*

DAY 1

1.

2.

3.

4.

5.

DAY 2

1.

2.

3.

4.

5.

DAY 3

1.

2.

3.

4.

5.

DAY 4

1.

2.

3.

4.

5.

DAY 5

1.

2.

3.

4.

5.

For the next five evenings, before bed, list five things you like about yourself.

EVENING   *I am...*

DAY 1

1.

2.

3.

4.

5.

DAY 2

1.

2.

3.

4.

5.

DAY 3

1.

2.

3.

4.

5.

DAY 4

1.

2.

3.

4.

5.

DAY 5

1.

2.

3.

4.

5.

6

Build from Sameness

Can you remember being in a relationship and saying, "It will never work, we are just too different."

News flash: opposites never attract. They only seem to because of the way each person behaves in relation to their needs.

For example, let's say the man you are dating has an underlying fear of abandonment. This causes him to have an exaggerated need to feel in control. He is aloof and won't commit. Having the same issue of abandonment, you also have a need to feel in control. In contrast to his behavior, you desire complete connection and commitment—and you want it fast.

This is only one example of behavior patterns based on the need to feel in control. A few other patterns are: a constant need for reassurance, consistently withholding information, having to know the other person's whereabouts at all times, and many variations thereof.

People in relationships are like in-ee and out-ee navels. They are the same, a belly button with the same purpose. They simply appear different.

Whatever your underlying needs are, Mr. Man has absolutely identical needs. You may have different behavior, but your needs will be identical. It is the behavior you use to hide your fear or express your love that is different, not the need itself.

It's not opposites attract, it's like seeks like.

The men you are attracted to are the ones that mirror you. They mirror your most innocent and intimate needs for love, approval, safety, and acceptance. Open yourself and do not be afraid to see yourself in those needs. From this open place you can build a relationship with Mr. Man.

Seeing Mr. Man with sameness allows you to approach him with the tools of curiosity, observation, and communication, which will provide you and him with a great sense of connection. This connection will move you past a relationship based on words into a relationship based on a connection of the heart.

Once established, a connection through the energy of the heart does not lead to self-protection, but to self-expression. It does not lead to regret, but to acceptance. It does not lead to expectations, but to giving—without attachment to an end result.

A heart connection is what we truly seek and it is our only true need. The heart connection is not an outcome, but rather a way of being.

The only path to a true connection of the heart is by seeing and building from sameness. You will feel safe, your defenses will go down, and true connection can begin.

Did you say, "It sounds too good to be true?" Not at all. In fact, it's easier.

It is so much easier on your psyche to address things in sameness—with curiosity, observation, and communication—than to expend huge amounts of energy fighting over differences and misunderstood context, not content.

Try a quick mind experiment. Imagine you and Mr. Man just had a big fight. He just doesn't understand what you need. Imagine it clearly. Take your time. Notice your mind as it fills with disappointment. You will find yourself depleted and confused that once again you have picked another bad apple. In a short time you will be depressed. And this was just your imagination.

Now revisit the same situation, and this time be open to your sameness. Envision that you are the same sock, just inside out and outside in. Can you see your comfort build as you recognize your similarities? In my experience, you will find yourself growing in energy, understanding, and excitement because you are learning something new.

Take the steps to see the sameness in you and your Mr. Man. Open your heart and connect. You and Mr. Man will be rewarded with a safe place to explore and create your relationship.

PRACTICE CURIOSITY

Practice the following exercise every day for the next five days. This exercise has two parts.

PART 1 *Ask Innocent Questions*

Remember when you where a child and you were curious about everything? You looked at the moon and wondered what kept it up in the sky? Why was Wednesday spelled so funny? Why did some people have curly hair and others straight?

Using this exercise, you are going to recapture that curious child. It's probably going to take some effort because most of us are conditioned to immediately agree or disagree, but seldom is anyone taught to be curious.

The first part of this practice is to ask lots of questions about everything. Remember to stay curious, and remember that true curiosity is always innocent. Do this everywhere and with everyone.

Innocence is very important. If you do not come from a place of innocence, people will sense they are being interrogated and clam up.

PART 2 *Eliminate Curiosity Eliminators*

The second part of this exercise is putting aside your "curiosity eliminators." When answering or asking a question, many people start their sentences with one of these three words: "yes," "but," or "no." You have probably done this several times today—or perhaps just now in your mind as you read this passage.

For this entire week of practicing curiosity, you are to replace yes, but, or no with the phrase, "That's interesting, may I ask you a question?"

You are not to start any sentence with yes, but, or no. You will really need to pay attention because yes, but, and no are so prevalent in our lives. Remember, only use, "That's interesting, may I ask you a question?" And mean it!

Be curious with everyone. Ask them about themselves, what they do, and why they do it.

A daily diet of curiosity will fill you with joy. It will lead you to learn more about Mr. Man and his sameness.

*For the next five mornings, before
you get out of bed, list six things
for which you are grateful.*

MORNING *I am grateful for...*

DAY 1

1. _____

_____

2. _____

_____

3. _____

_____

4. _____

_____

5. _____

_____

6. _____

_____

DAY 2

1.

2.

3.

4.

5.

6.

DAY 3

1.

2.

3.

4.

5.

6.

DAY 4

1.

2.

3.

4.

5.

6.

DAY 5

1.

2.

_____

_____

3.

_____

_____

4.

_____

_____

5.

_____

_____

6.

_____

_____

> For the next five evenings, before
> bed, list six things you like about
> yourself.

EVENING *I am...*

1.

2.

3.

4.

5.

6.

DAY 2

1. _____

_____

2. _____

_____

3. _____

_____

4. _____

_____

5. _____

_____

6. _____

_____

DAY 3

1. _____

_____

2. _____

_____

3. _____

_____

4.

5.

6.

DAY 4

1.

2.

3.

4.

5.

6.

DAY 5

1.

2.

3.

4.

5.

6.

7

Never, Ever Fight

When you cross the line from conversation to arguing and then to fighting, you enter the land of destruction. If you want a man to stick around, never ever fight with him. This needs to be said again. If you want your man, never, ever fight.

Fighting is the coup de grace, the biggest of all no-nos. When you fight, you are trying to make the other person wrong. It is merciless annihilation, for power that does not exist to begin with. Fighting is destruction without construction. It is knocking down the house to expand the room.

Fighting is usually the result of pent-up emotions looking for a release, and it is seldom about the circumstances that stimulate it. Fighting never truly addresses the underlying cause, but rather it pokes at it, opening old wounds that are not about the present day. The resulting "make up," if there is one, never produces a lasting result because the underlying issue is still there, waiting for the next opportunity to express itself inappropriately.

Fighting is the ultimate projection. It is seeking power over another because you fear you are less valuable than that person. It leads you to paint all your past negative emotions onto Mr. Man. When you are projecting negative emotions, intimacy, trust, love, and all the other hallmarks of a true relationship are impossible. This is because you are interacting with your past and not the person in front of you.

When you feel a need to spar, find out what is driving your behavior. Check out the energy rising in you: the indignation, the judgment, and the condemnation. Use curiosity to solicit your Objective Viewer to find out what lies beneath the energy. Do so even if your curiosity sounds like, "What the *bleep* am I doing?"

What lies beneath the need to fight can be revealed and then healed if you focus on it. It is an illusion that a fight will discharge negative energy. In fact, fighting multiplies negative energy.

Arguing is different than fighting. Arguing is belief systems revealed. Fighting is emotional problems revealed. Arguing is being in the present time. Fighting is being in the past.

When you argue, you disagree with another person, but respect their right to their opinion. You don't make them wrong to make yourself right. You just don't see things the same—and that is actually an asset. What a small boring world we would live in if everyone saw things the same way.

To make a point, or to argue, is like experiencing a birth pain. It is a sign of two people bringing to the surface belief systems that they are trying to see in a bigger manner.

The pattern of an argument may resemble the following: While holding your partner in unconditional positive regard and approaching him with curiosity, you parade your thoughts. Then you wait for a comment. If your partner disagrees, you make your case as to why you believe in what you said. If your case holds up in his vision, you feel happy that you have investigated your thoughts and they were unanimously seen as good.

If your partner disagrees with your position, you debate the thought, trying on each other's perspective. On a good night, you come to understand both perspectives. Like two instruments playing in harmony, together you create a new concerto.

At the very least you can parade your thoughts and he can parade his. These may not be remotely the same thought, but you can respect each other and agree to disagree. Disagreement is not unhealthy.

To be with a man with whom you can open your thoughts for agreement or disagreement, and see a bigger picture, is amazing. This type of relationship is worth striving for.

As a relationship policy, always agree to disagree respectfully.

If you find yourself trying to win Mr. Man over to your point of view, and you feel judgment of his opinion slipping in, take note—you are headed for a fight. Likewise, if you see him trying to win *you* over to his point of view and you feel judgment of your opinion slipping in, you are headed for a fight.

In that moment, stop, re-sync, and think to yourself, "Don't destroy. Build." Then, say to Mr. Man, "Let's agree to disagree."

PROPAGATE YOUR PREVIOUS GOOD FEELINGS

Practice the following exercise every day for the next five days.

Remember the last time you slipped into the (metaphoric) boxing ring, ready to take on your opponent? See the scene, watch it unfold, and let the aftermath run. Do you remember what you felt and the damage it caused?

Would you like to find a different way to express yourself, one where your point may actually be heard and accepted? Yes?

First, stand up and shake any emotion out of your body. Then, sit down and clear your mind. If you have a problem clearing your mind, use the following imagery: Picture yourself sitting on the side of a flowing river. There are sticks floating down the river. Theses sticks are your thoughts floating by. Let them float away.

Scan your history and think of a time you felt good about yourself, a time when you felt on top of the world, in the moment and clear-minded. This could have been getting a promotion, fitting into your jeans, closing a deal, or generally having a good hair day. What did it feel like, look like, smell like? Is it associated with a place? Remember it well.

Once you have good feelings established, go back to the memory of the fight and see yourself in that situation along with those good feelings. See the outcome of the fight change. It can't stay the same because you aren't the same.

Repeat the scene with all the good feelings three times. Each time, make the scene brighter, warmer, and more joyous.

Next, with these same feelings of warmth and joy, imagine yourself in a future event that could lead to a fight. See yourself with your clear-minded, good feelings of being present and in the moment. See the potential for a fight evaporate. Do this future rehearsal three times.

You can use a different fight from your past each day.

You are practicing who you want to be. It was practice that perfected your behavior of fighting, and practice is the way your behavior will change.

For the next five mornings, before
you get out of bed, list seven
things for which you are grateful.

MORNING   *I am grateful for...*

DAY 1

1.

2.

3.

4.

5.

6.

7.

DAY 2

1. _____

2. _____

3. _____

4. _____

5. _____

6. _____

7. _____

DAY 3

1. _____

2. _____

3.

4.

5.

6.

7.

DAY 4

1.

2.

3.

4.

5.

6.

_____

_____

7.

_____

_____

DAY 5

1.

_____

_____

2.

_____

_____

3.

_____

_____

4.

_____

_____

5.

_____

_____

6.

_____

_____

7.

_____

_____

For the next five evenings, before bed, list seven things you like about yourself.

EVENING   *I am...*

DAY 1

1. _____

_____

2. _____

_____

3. _____

_____

4. _____

_____

5. _____

_____

6. _____

_____

7. _____

DAY 2

1.

2.

3.

4.

5.

6.

7.

DAY 3

1.

2.

3.

4.

5.

6.

7.

DAY 4

1.

2.

3.

4.

5.

6.
_____

_____

7.
_____

_____

DAY 5

1.
_____

_____

2.
_____

_____

3.
_____

_____

4.
_____

_____

5.
_____

_____

6.
_____

_____

7.
_____

_____

8

Embrace Change

C hange in a relationship is constant. It is the one thing you can absolutely count on, whether you want it or not. But your thoughts about relationships are often static, set in stone by your childhood role models, including your parents, culture, and so forth. This static condition of what you think relationships are supposed to be is in conflict with what relationships actually are. This causes you to resist the natural change in relationships.

No matter how much change you have experienced, parts of you stay attached to establishing an illusory safe place that does not change. You could say that these parts of you are designed to detect and resist change.

When these parts feel change approaching, they create emotions to avoid or control the change. These emotions and behaviors are generated by experiences where change often equaled pain. These unhappy outcomes were generally out of your control, such as parents getting divorced, moving, losing a pet, or changing schools.

Change-resistant aspects of your psyche will attempt to protect you from experiencing the pain of change. Unfortunately, the emotional and behavioral tool set these parts of you use for protection will sabotage your relationships in the process.

In the name of keeping you safe, these emotions and resulting behavior can cause you to leave relationships that are about to become bigger, greater, or deeper. Conversely, your protective aspects can influence you to stay in relationships that are no longer in your best interest just because they are predictable.

This is child-driven behavior, which is in direct conflict with the adult you who needs movement and growth. Without embracing the natural change in your relationship, you will unconsciously create change to bring excitement, sometimes in the form of drama, to your life.

What is needed is skill in managing your emotions about relationship changes. Many people don't have this skill. They let their emotions run loose, saying and doing whatever comes to mind. Other people hold their emotions back, repressing them until they feel like victims.

It is natural to have emotions about change in relationships, but you must become the captain of them. Use your emotions as excitement to embrace the expansion and contraction of change.

Here is an example of poorly-handled change: You find the love of your life, your Mr. Man. You and he feel natural together, and natural feels safe. After several months of intense connection, Mr. Man begins to withdraw. You don't understand why, and he is not talking. Mr. Man has changed.

Your emotions come out saying, "It must mean blank!" In that moment, your un-captained emotions frantically try to recapture a feeling of comfort and safety. This results in demanding behavior. You want to know why he is backing off. You push him for an answer, and if you don't get one, you will try a different tactic, perhaps backing off and becoming indifferent. Mr. Man starts to think, "Does she love me or am I just someone filling a role?"

After you travel through a challenging emotional landscape, you find out you made an assumption. In reality, he was only preoccupied with work. You say, "If you had just told me, I would not have responded in such a manner." All the while you are thinking, "If I knew this change was temporary I could have managed my emotions. All I wanted to know was that it was safe and your love for me would not change."

He says, "Why don't you trust me?" All the while he is thinking, "If I told you this change was temporary, I would never have known if you loved me. I wanted to know that it was safe and your love for me would not change."

You are both looking for the same thing. In this case, you don't want the other person to change.

Don't confuse the natural state of change in a relationship with losing sight of yourself. Women often change their hair, makeup, style of dress, career, car and house because they believe that their Mr. Man would prefer less, brighter, smarter, more, you name it.

This is called contortion. It's an unhealthy thing to do.

Contortion is an attempt to activate Mr. Man's feelings for you in a positive direction. Sometimes contortion is obvious, but often you can't see yourself doing it. These changes are made with the expectation that Mr. Man will accept, love and value you more if you make them.

You can change yourself for love, but the love has to be *for yourself*. If you change for a man, that change is temporary. It only lasts until you get what you want. Invariably you won't want what you get and then you blame Mr. Man for causing your contortion.

First, you become like a chameleon, changing yourself for approval, and then you become like a tarantula, killing your mate after copulation.

The natural state of relationships is expansion and contraction. This is how you were born into the world and it is how you will birth yourself into new aspects of your relationship with yourself and Mr. Man.

You need to fall in love over and over again in the same relationship by embracing the natural state of change.

OBSERVATION OF CHANGE

Practice the following exercise every day for the next five days.

Simple observation of how much change goes on in your day will help you reprogram your subconscious to accept that change is natural and okay. Here is an imaginary observation of both small and big changes.

The first change of the day is that you wake up. You have just changed from being asleep to being awake.

You go to your closet and pick something to wear, and you don't wear the same clothes as yesterday.

On your way to work, there is lots of traffic so you change your route. At work, you can't park in your regular place, so you change your parking location.

Once at your desk, you receive an unexpected telephone call from a recruiter who offers you a career opportunity with an increase in your pay and position. This is very timely because you just got a notice that the company is downsizing.

You have vacation plans with your best friend. She calls to tell you her work schedule has changed and she has to cancel the four-day trip to the Bahamas. The project she is on will send her to Paris for three months. She will have some time off in Paris during the time frame of your original vacation, so you can meet her and stay for free. The only thing you have to pay for is your airline ticket, which she can get at a reduced rate.

Great fantasy.

Now, for the next five days observe yourself and all the changes you make all day, every day. The more you observe, the more you will realize you can and do survive change. And change often brings rewards.

If you find yourself in overload, reacting to change rather than responding or adapting to it, take a minute and talk to the part of you that is uncomfortable or even afraid.

First, "Normafy" the moment you are in by using the You-Niversal Remote to fast-forward past your emotions (see pages 61, 62, 63 and 64).

Second, when you have a quiet space, Infinite Possibilities (see pages 33, 34 and 35). See yourself float back in time and explain to that part of you how many changes big and small you have both survived. Remind her how some changes led to fun, happiness, love, awareness, and growth.

Before long, your anxiety will turn to excitement in the face of the unknown change. Embrace change. After all, Mr. Man may be waiting for you in Paris.

For the next five mornings, before
you get out of bed, list eight
things for which you are grateful.

MORNING *I am grateful for...*

DAY 1

1.

2.

3.

4.

5.

6.

7.

8.

DAY 2

1.

2.

3.

4.

5.

6.

7.

8.

DAY 3

1.

2.

3.

4.

5.

6.

7.

8.

DAY 4

1.

2.

3.

4.

5.

6.

7.

8.

DAY 5

1.

2.

3.

4.

5.

6.

7.

8.

For the next five evenings, before bed, list eight things you like about yourself.

EVENING *I am...*

DAY 1

1. _____

_____

2. _____

_____

3. _____

_____

4. _____

_____

5. _____

_____

6. _____

_____

7. _____

8.

DAY 2

1.

2.

3.

4.

5.

6.

7.

8.

DAY 3

1.

2.

3.

4.

5.

6.

7.

8.

DAY 4

1.

2.

3.

4.

5.

6.

7.

8.

DAY 5

1.

2.

3.

4.

_____

_____

5.

_____

_____

6.

_____

_____

7.

_____

_____

8.

_____

_____

9

Find Your No

In the cause and effect world, relationships have been primarily based on commerce. "You bring me the bear and I sleep with you" has now turned into, "You bring me the Mercedes and I sleep with you."

Sometime in the 1940s, a shift in consciousness to become whole began. The roles we once played began to change. Women went to work in untold numbers and the paradigm of "you-man, you-hunt" and "me-woman, I-stay-home" went out the door.

This shift involved more than just women working or not working. We shifted as Spirits. Our yin began its journey home to join with our yang. Until this shift, men held the root and women held the heart. Men have had their "I and me" and now they are coming into their "we." Women have had their "we and me" and are coming into their "I."

This profound global shift in personal energies is affecting our relationships. The old roles are gone. We are moving into a space where each individual in a relationship is a whole integrated person, not two halves trying to make a whole. However, old roles die slowly and we can still find commerce in our relationships. "You bring home the bear and I will have sex with you" is still loosely present.

Attachment to gaining a man's approval is a sure sign that we have not moved into our wholeness, and that we are separated from ourselves. From this approval-based mindset, we develop controlling behavior patterns that are based on getting what we want.

We think the behavior we use to get what we want is love, but in fact it is not an expression of love; it is an attempt to gain control. Once we give a man our body, we want him to care, share, and be there for us. We use sex to close the deal. If we can't sleep with Mr. Man out of love, letting go of all conditions, we shouldn't do it—or we should do it knowing that it is commerce.

Commerce in sex is prostitution; it doesn't matter the means of payment. We have all been prostitutes, men and women selling ourselves to have our needs met.

We must say "no" to relationship commerce. If you are having trouble determining whether your relationship is based on commerce, you can easily make an assessment. A telltale sign of relationship commerce is the inability to say and hear "no."

Women are notorious for hearing a man's "no" as a personal insult. They have linked it to a lack of respect. For example, Mr. Man invites you to attend a lecture on his favorite subject. You have no interest in attending the lecture. You can't find your no; so you say "yes." He thinks he did something nice by including you. You think you did something nice by attending.

In this scenario, however, your attendance comes with an expectation of reciprocation. If Mr. Man doesn't reciprocate for your act of pseudo-kindness, his choice stimulates the following reactions: "He is just a selfish ass." "After all I do for him he should do this for me and with joy." "He must not care for me."

First, you brew resentment for doing the things you don't want to do, then you brew resentment for the things you think he should do. And then you judge him based on the implied contract of reciprocation that he was never privy to in the first place.

The resentment and judgment you feel when Mr. Man breaks your fantasy contract comes from wanting payback for your faux good deeds. You are looking for validation that you are worthy, valuable, or lovable enough to commit to. His participation or non-participation in your fantasy-designed reciprocation contract does not have anything to do with your worth, value, or lovability.

When you give with expectation, you will get angry when your expectations are not met.

As women, we have contorted ourselves for centuries with a need to be approved by giving a lifetime of false yeses. We must give ourselves the right to say "no" to doing what we truly don't want to do.

Without the ability to say and hear "no" without judgment, there is no true "yes."

When we develop our no-yes power, relationship commerce goes away. Then we have an opportunity to create a relationship from our self-awareness and merge our body with another soul to express being Love.

DOOR OF TRANSFORMATION

Practice the following exercise every day for the next five days.

Look at yourself as pure energy. You are 100 percent energy, and this energy goes where you direct it.

At present, your energy is often directed outward. You project it away from yourself to create your reality. Your experiences have energy connected to three major groups of desire—safety, value, and authority—in the form of sub-desires, such as longing, trust, and need.

Over the course of your life, you have taken your life force, your Spirit, and projected it onto different people, places, things, and organizations in order to bring what you think you desire into your reality. The problem is that people, places, things, and organizations don't have the ability to provide this for you. The good news is you have the ability to provide this for yourself, turning what you desire into reality.

But how do you create when your energy bank is half full? You can't, at least not effectively, efficiently, or in any lasting way. People can't create until they have called back the energy they have projected. Until then, they are in repetition.

Use this exercise to call back your energy from the people, places, things, or organizations you have projected it on and to direct it for your own personal creation.

Read the following instructions several times. Then follow them as closely as possible from memory.

Locate yourself in a very relaxing, quiet place. Then, close your eyes.

See yourself as if you were in the center of a room. This is your room, and it looks and feels like it. On the walls, ceiling, and floor are pictures of all the different events and relationships of your life.

Imagine your energy coming from the inside of your body, projecting outward to the scenes that best represent your efforts to produce safety, value and authority.

Now, with your mind's eye, see yourself pulling your energy back into your body through a door. This is your Door of Transformation, a mechanism that transforms your experiences into wisdom and clarity. As your energy passes through the Door of Transformation, any negative emotions, thoughts, feelings, or pain you feel from your experiences releases itself into sheer divine life force untainted and untarnished. Your energy streams back to you through the door as wisdom, clarity, and divine life force—full of possibility and potential—see your body fill with the energy.

As your energy returns to your body, notice a gauge that tells you when your energy has reached 100 percent. When the gauge has reached "full," close your door firmly, and put your focus on the energy flowing through your body. Doesn't it feel great to have a full tank?

Take your transformed energy and extend it from your body through the top of your head straight out to the center of the universe. When your energy has reached the center of the universe, see the universe open to a sacred place, a place where your divine spirit is connected to you.

See your energy anchored into this nirvana, this Shangri-La, this heaven, creating a portal from your body to the center of the universe. Surrounding your energy is your Wise Council of Spirit. See your Wise Council send your energy back down to your body reinforced in its divine potential and possibility.

Keep your portal open and anchored to this divine place. Feel your energy tingle and spark as it returns to your body gleaming with love and potential.

Now, see your energy flow through your root into the center of Mother Earth. See yourself anchored into this nirvana, this Shangri-La, this heaven, creating a portal from the center of the universe through your body into the center of Mother Earth. Surrounding your energy is your Earthly Wise Council of Spirit. See your Earthly Wise Council send your energy back up to your body reinforced in its earthly potential and possibility.

Keep your portal open and anchored to this divine place. Feel your energy return to your body from Mother Earth, flowing and free, creating a great sense of comfort and safety. Clear like water. Feel your body fill with the flow.

With your body filled with this flow, see a blank white card in front of you. Write a positive statement on the card. Write down what you desire to create in your life. It might be: "I am whole, I am strong, I am loving, I am harmonious, I am happy, I am healthy." You can also be very specific. "I am a size *blank*. I weigh blank. I achieve this by blank, I create this now."

As soon as you have written what you want to manifest, stamp your face on the card and send it back up to the center of the universe where you are anchored. See your Wise Council of Spirit transform the card into the energy to achieve your desire. Watch it return to you and enter your body. Feel the sparkle. Notice that it may feel different every time you do it.

See the energy flow down through your root and into Mother Earth, the center of the earth where it turns into a seed. See your Earthly Wise Council grow that seed into energy returning back to you through your root chakra, where it begins to expand itself into your body. See the energy of your creation turn into a magnetic field that emanates from your skin.

You are now manifesting your desire.

For the next five mornings, before
you get out of bed, list nine
things for which you are grateful.

MORNING *I am grateful for...*

DAY 1

1. _____
_____

2. _____
_____

3. _____
_____

4. _____
_____

5. _____
_____

6. _____
_____

7. _____

8.

9.

DAY 2

1.

2.

3.

4.

5.

6.

7.

8.

9.

DAY 3

1.

2.

3.

4.

5.

6.

7.

8.

9.

DAY 4

1.

2.

4.

3.

5.

6.

7.

8.

9.

DAY 5

1.

2.

3.

4.

5.

6.

7.

8.

9.

For the next five evenings, before bed, list nine things you like about yourself.

EVENING   *I am...*

DAY 1

1.

2.

3.

4.

5.

6.

7.

8.

9.

DAY 2

1.

2.

3.

4.

5.

6.

7.

8.

9.

DAY 3

1.

2.

3.

4.

5.

6.

7.

8.

9.

DAY 4

1.

2.

4.

3.

5.

6.

7.

8.

9.

DAY 5

1.

2.

3.

4.

5.

6.

7.

8.

9.

10

See the Divine in Yourself and Others

For the past nine weeks you have looked at yourself and your behavior. Using new tools, you gained new insights to change your relationship life.

A theme repeated throughout this book is connecting back to the real you, with no static or interference.

You have one real relationship in this world—and that relationship is with your divinity, the essence of the true you. When that relationship is held as the dearest and most important in your life, you can have a healthy relationship with anyone. Your external relationships will reflect your wonderful first relationship with your divinity.

You are infinite and incomprehensible, but fully discoverable. If you embrace this truth, you will see yourself without judgment, holding your amazing life in high regard and curiosity. When you are in awareness of your essence, you see your experiences as a movie you have written and directed. This state of awareness is your True Self.

The True Self knows love because it is Love. This is where you will find relationship communion, commonality, equality, respect, and all the other virtues for which you have been looking. You have learned they do not exist in the past experiences you cobbled together as your identity. They exist in the realization of your oneness with the Creator.

Once aligned with your True Self, you can see your Mr. Man as a divine being. You will see his divinity whether he is in a moment of True Self or whether he is responding or reacting to a movie he has written.

Maybe you are thinking, "Cynthia, I am just trying to get a man. I don't want to be overwhelmed by trying to be an attribute of the Creator."

You don't have to *try* to be an attribute of the Creator. You already *are* an attribute of the Creator. Remember you are made in the image and likeness of the Creator. You are what the Creator is. It is as simple as that. You are either aware of your divinity are you are unaware of your divinity. Your divinity is there regardless of your perception of it.

You can be mesmerized and hypnotized by your experiences, or you can see them as your creations with the meaning you assign them.

So it ain't hard.

You have tried it many other ways and the reason you are reading this book is because they didn't work. So now you have *The 10 Ways*:

1. Own Your Behavior
2. Create a New Value System
3. Start with Self-Communication
4. Commit to Living Your Life
5. Pick Your Time
6. Build from Sameness
7. Never, Ever Fight

8. Embrace Change

9. Find Your No

10. See the Divine in Yourself and Others

The next time you find yourself dissatisfied or bewildered, let yourself go into the flow. Close your eyes. See your life as a choice, see yourself as limitless possibilities, and see yourself as infinite. Take a moment and hold yourself in absolutely unconditional positive regard. The love you feel for yourself will fill the room. Then look at your partner the same way.

Think of love as a state of grace, not a means to anything, but the alpha and omega, an end in itself.

—Gabriel Gárcia Márquez

Your ability to be a woman—whole, genuine, loving, creative, self-aware, and sexual—comes from being Love. Being Love has no alternative except to produce love in your world.

We get love by being Love.

And this, my little chickiepoo, is how to live the 21st century relationship.

Last, but most important, we would like the last words in this book to be yours. It's your book of life, your individual journey.

List ten attributes of the Creator:

1. _____

2. _____

4. _____

3. _____

5. _____

6. _____

7. _____

8. _____

9.

_____

_____

10.

_____

_____

Now, put your name next to each one.

> *Remember, the source and*
> *the substance are one.*

www.ingramcontent.com/pod-product-compliance
Lightning Source LLC
Chambersburg PA
CBHW052356090426
42739CB00011B/2394